Praise for *Get That Book Published!*

"In *Get That Book Published!* Lana Castle has produced a volume that is jam packed with step-by-step information on how to navigate the bewildering world of publishing. An accomplished author, Ms. Castle knows what she's talking about. Aspiring writers can do themselves a favor and jumpstart their careers by following this easy-to-read guide."

> – Sheila Allee, Executive Director, Writers' League of Texas and author of *Seven Steps to the Podium: A Concise Handbook for Speakers and Speechwriters* and *Texas Mutiny: Bullets, Ballads and Boss Rule*

"Follow Lana. If you want to be published, she gives you the choices short and sweet. Whether you follow your heart or your pocketbook, this book furnishes direction. With Lana's help, I self-published *Honk If You Married Sonja*. I'm proud of my book. Read *Get That Book Published!* and make the best decision. It doesn't matter where you are in the writing process. This book is for you."

> – Sonja Klein, author of *Honk If You Married Sonja: The Travels and Essays of Sonja Klein*

"*Get That Book Published!* is an extremely informative guide that chronicles the various pathways to get published. From traditional to self-publishing, and hardcover to ebook, Lana Castle spells it all out as she covers every aspect of this mysterious, often crazy business. Don't stumble through it the hard way like I did; save yourself a lot of time and effort by reading this book!"

> – Thomas M. Earnhart, author of *Mars Base Delta and the Medusa Stone*

"This book takes a lot of the mystery out of the process of writing and publishing a book. In a friendly, no-nonsense way, Lana Castle walks you capably through the many decisions an author-to-be faces — all without making it more complicated than it has to be. Clear writing, diagrams, illustrations and concise chapters make this book a valuable field guide for the library of anyone considering writing a book."

– Patti DeNucci, author of *The Intentional Networker: Attracting Powerful Relationships, Referrals & Results in Business*

"*Get That Book Published!* is user-friendly and a wonderfully organized guide to the entire spectrum of book publishing. It is a very useful and important book which should be in the hands of every aspiring writer. I highly recommend it!"

– Edward T. Martin, author of *King of Travelers, Jesus' Lost Years in India*

Get That Book Published!

A Roadmap for Today's Writer

by

Lana R. Castle

Get That Book Published! A Roadmap for Today's Writer

Copyright 2012 by Lana R. Castle

International Standard Book Numbers

Kindle
ISBN-10: 0-9662926-3-4
ISBN-13: 978-0-9662926-3-3

Other Ebook Formats (through Smashwords)
ISBN-10: 0-9662926-4-2
ISBN-13: 978-0-9662926-4-0

Softcover
ISBN-10: 0-9662926-2-6
ISBN-13: 978-0-9662926-2-6

Printed in the United States of America

Castle Communications
3900 Balcones Woods Drive
Austin, TX 78759-5006
512-413-5059
www.castlecommunications.com

* * *

*For every writer —
experienced, new or "wannabe" —
who wants to learn more about
today's publishing pathways*

* * *

CONTENTS

CONTENTS (continued)

THE EBOOK PUBLISHING PATHWAY

1

INTRODUCTION

Want to get a book published? Great! *Get That Book Published!* describes three different pathways you might follow to do just that. For each pathway, this book also explains the "pit stops" a book makes to get printed and/or become an ebook and get into a reader's hands. These pathways include:

• Publishing a printed book through traditional publishing,

• Self-publishing a printed book through an offset printer, a digital printer or a print-on-demand (POD) company and

• Self-publishing an electronic or digital book (ebook).

These pathways need not necessarily be mutually exclusive. For instance, you might self-publish a book in either print or electronic form — or both — and later publish that same book through a traditional publisher.

No particular pathway is better than another. The ideal pathway or pathways vary with each author and each book. I have published my own books through both a traditional publisher and through self-publishing. I chose my approach based on my goals for each book. My clients have used a variety of publishing options as well. Each approach has its advantages and disadvantages. *Get That Book Published!* points them out and helps you decide on the best pathway or pathways for you and your books. So let's get going!

The table of contents and following flowcharts illustrate the stops along each pathway. I know they look a *bit* complex, but *please don't panic!* I'll explain everything along the way.

The Traditional Publishing Pathway

Query/Proposal

Agent

Publisher

Manuscript

Designer, Layout Artist, Photographer

CONTRACT

Editor

Distributor

Printer/Conversion Service

Your Book!

Promotion

Meet the Author!

BOOKS

Bookstore/Library

Your Book!

Ebook

Direct Sales

Income/Royalties

2

QUERY & PROPOSAL

When you think about publishing, you may first think about traditional publishing. Most writers do. Traditional publishing offers the most prestige and often the highest quality and widest distribution. Traditional publishers tend to have more funds to invest in large, high-quality print runs than self-publishers do. And since most publishers pay an advance, you often get more income. Once you've sold enough books for the publisher to recoup your advance, you get royalties.

However, traditional publishing usually takes a lot of time. You may have to find a good literary agent or do a lot of research to find the right publisher. Then once you land a contract, your book will usually be one among many books needing the publisher's resources.

To get published by a traditional publisher — especially if this is your first book — start by writing a complete rough draft.

Once your draft is complete, send a query letter to a potential agent *or* to an editor who works for a publisher that accepts unsolicited (unagented) work. Also submit any other materials their guidelines suggest. (See chapters 3 and 4.)

Querying more than one agent or editor at a time is fine — but only if those agents or editors accept simultaneous submissions and you tell them that's what you're doing.

For fiction, you'll usually need a query letter, a synopsis and either the first 3 polished chapters or a complete polished manuscript. Sometimes you can skip a formal book proposal.

For nonfiction, you'll usually need a query letter, a book proposal and either 1–3 chapters or a complete manuscript.

For a memoir, you'll usually need a query letter, a book proposal and a complete polished manuscript.

Some content suggestions follow. The text in brackets indicates information you should fill in. The formatting information is for regular mail. When you send email, use the same content but don't try to center text or set it flush right.

When you send regular mail, always enclose an SASE (self-addressed, stamped envelope). Don't use dated metered postage on the SASE; otherwise, you may never get a response. If the agent or editor you're approaching accepts emailed queries or synopses, omit the line that reads "Enc.: SASE." Send the query or synopsis in the email itself rather than as an attachment. Many people won't open attachments they aren't expecting.

When sending a book proposal, sample chapters or a complete manuscript, send a copy by regular mail unless the agent or editor requests an electronic copy. Send sample chapters and complete drafts unbound and in standard manuscript format. I'll show you that soon.

Book Query Letter

[Your Name]
[Street or PO Box]
[City, State, Zip]
[Phone *(with area code)*]
[Email address]

The point of a query letter is to get a literary agent or an editor at a traditional publishing house interested in your book. Make it brief (preferably one page), enticing and professional. Use letterhead or plain white or off-white paper.

[Date — *About 4 lines below your address information*]

[Specific Agent/Editor's Name]
[Agency/Publisher]
[Street or PO Box]
[City, State, Zip]

Skip 2–4 lines

Dear [Specific Agent/Editor's Name]:

Stimulate interest in your book with a one-sentence hook that reveals the book's main idea. Summarize the book in 1–3 sentences without revealing its conclusion. Include the book's proposed title and genre and the approximate word — not page — count.

Discuss the need for your book, what makes it unique and why readers will be interested. Define your market(s).

Introduce yourself and your expertise as it relates to the book. If you haven't published anything, don't mention it or apologize.

If you wish, tell why you chose to submit to that particular agent/editor. Personalize it.

Request permission to send a book proposal/synopsis and 1–3 sample chapters or a complete manuscript — whatever the guidelines suggest. Mention whether you are querying other agents/editors as well.

[Closing],

Write your signature.

[Your Name]

Enc.: SASE — *Be sure you enclose it!*

Novel Synopsis

1–1.5" margin, double-space text

1–1.5" margin — *Use one side only of plain white paper and an ordinary 12-point font like Times New Roman. Write 1–5 pages, as if you're telling a story.* — 1–1.5" margin

[Your Name]   [Genre]
[Contact information]   [Approximate word count — *figure*
                                          as 250 words per standard double-
[Agent's Name (if represented)]   *spaced manuscript page]*
[Contact information]

[TITLE]
in all caps, 16–18 lines from top

SYNOPSIS
followed by 4–6 lines before text

[Hook] — *Stimulate the reader's interest and promise action.*

[Setting] — *Introduce the date, time and place.*

[Main characters] — *Introduce by name [all caps on first mention], age, short physical description, traits, goals and career.*

[Secondary characters] — *Briefly describe them and contrast them with the main characters.*

[Plot & crisis point] — *Briefly summarize the conflict, major plot points and crisis, as if telling the story.*

[Resolution] — *State how the story ends.*

---

page 2 and following pages

1–1.5" margin, double-space text

1–1.5" margin — [Your Name]/[Shortened Book Title]   Synopsis/[Page number] — 1–1.5" margin

2–3 blank lines to text

Standard Book Manuscript Format

1-1.5" margin, double-space text

1-1.5"
margin

Use one side only of plain white paper and an ordinary 12-point font like Times New Roman.

1-1.5"
margin

[Your Name]   [Genre]
[Street or PO Box]   [Approximate word count — *figure*
[City, State, Zip]   *as 250 words per standard double-*
[Phone *(with area code)*]   *spaced manuscript page*]
[Email address]

[TITLE]
In all caps, 16-18 lines from top, followed by 4-6 lines

by [Your Name]
followed by 4-6 lines before text

[Body starts here.] *Double-space the entire body. Start with a strong hook that will grab the reader's attention and encourage him or her to read on.*

Indent the first line of each paragraph by .25-.5 inch.

1-1.5" margin

---

page 2 and following pages

1-1.5" margin, double-space text

1-1.5"
margin

[Your Name]/[Shortened Book Title]   [Page number]

1-1.5"
margin

3-4 blank lines to text

Paragraph continues flush left or a new, indented paragraph starts.

U.S. copyright law instantly covers anything you write, and a traditional publisher will register your copyright for you. If you wish, though, you can copyright your manuscript on your own. Go to www.copyright.gov.

Don't include a copyright notice on your manuscript — it looks amateurish, and publishing people do know the law.

Mark the end of manuscript with –30– or ### as shown below.

###

1-1.5" margin

Book Proposal Contents

A book proposal should contain the following elements:

Cover Letter [1–2 pages] — Address this to a specific agent or editor who's expressed interest in seeing your work.

Title Page — Type "Book Proposal" in the upper left corner and center your proposed title and byline (your name). List your contact information and your agent's contact information, if you have an agent, at the bottom of the page. (Chapter 3 discusses ways to get an agent.)

Table of Contents — For your proposal, not for the book itself.

Overview [1-2 pages] — Introduce your book's concept. Describe the specific potential audience(s). "Everybody" or "the general public" is *not* specific enough! Tell why your book is needed, what it will accomplish and what makes it interesting, timely and unique.

Competition — List the top five or six books in the marketplace that compete with or relate to yours, and explain how yours is different without saying yours is better. Research your competition thoroughly by going to bookstores, searching online and checking Bowker's *Books in Print*.

Marketing Plan — [2–3 pages] — I can't overstress the importance of this section. It's a must-have to get a traditional publisher. In your marketing plan:

1. Estimate the size of your target audience(s). Cite statistics if possible.

2. Explain what you will do to market your book, using connections and strategies you already have in place.

3. Tell how you'll use your website and/or other resources and how it/they will link to the publisher and/or to booksellers.

4. List any distribution avenues you already have in place for people to buy books. (Mass sales to companies, organizations, specialty stores and so on.)

5. List any people who have already committed to endorse your book (upon approval of the manuscript).

Delivery — Specify the approximate word count and the number of tables, illustrations, photos, forms, appendices, etc., plus whether you've obtained permission to use them. Sometimes you can use previously published pieces for free, but often you'll have to pay for the privilege.

Chapter Outline *for nonfiction* [1–3 paragraphs per chapter] — Describe each chapter in an inviting way. Send a **Synopsis** *for fiction* [1–5 pages] — *But follow the guidelines.*

Author Bio [1 page]

1. Explain why you are the authority to write this book.

2. State your credentials (include education, awards, organizations and leadership positions).

3. Mention your publishing experience, if you have some. If you haven't been published, don't mention it or apologize.

Audience — Describe any built-in audience you have through writing, speaking, blogging, media exposure and the like. This is called your "platform."

Sample Chapters [1–3] — The first chapter and other representative chapters for nonfiction. Usually the first three chapters or up to 50 pages for fiction. *Follow the guidelines.*

SASE — Again, use stamps only, not metered postage. Include instructions about what you do or don't need back.

Warning: Never send an original! Send a photocopy or an electronic file that you've backed up. This goes for text, tables, illustrations, photos, forms and so on.

3

AGENT

If you want a traditional publisher, you'll likely need a literary agent. A literary agent's most important job is to match you and your book to the most appropriate publisher and to help you negotiate a good contract.

Many writers meet their agents at writers' conferences. Some get referrals from published associates. Others find an agent by email or regular mail. In any case, it pays to do your homework first.

Check agents' websites, www.PublishersMarketplace.com or the *Writer's Digest Guide to Literary Agents*. These sources list the types of books that agents represent, what they want you to submit and how they prefer to be approached.

Don't send your book proposal, synopsis or manuscript unless an agent requests it. *And don't send any unpolished work!* Spell check, grammar check and proofread *everything* thoroughly before you send it out. Make it as professional as possible. Publishing is a *business*, and successful writers must be businesslike.

Warning: Be wary of agents who approach you first. They're often more interested in collecting reading and editing fees than in representing authors and their books. Avoid agents who charge for anything other than small incidentals such as photocopies and postage. Most agents get 15% of an author's advance and royalties, and that's all.

Reputable agents tend to be members of the Association of Authors' Representatives. Good agents will tell you what authors they represent, what other books they have sold and which publishers they have worked with. You can also ask for references from their other authors. Choose your agent carefully.

If your book happens to be published internationally, you may need a second agent to negotiate foreign contracts. Your primary agent will probably already have a relationship with one and will deal with him or her directly.

If the foreign rights agent sells your book to a publisher in another country, both agents get a commission for the deal. The commissions come out of what the foreign publisher pays you for the right to publish your book in that country. Even a small commission is well worth it because a foreign contract requires no further work on your part. It's icing on the cake!

Another important part of a literary agent's job is to keep on top of book sales and send you payments from the publisher.

4

PUBLISHER

The publisher is the company or person responsible for getting a book produced. Traditional publishers pay you for the right to publish your book and also pay most of the expenses for getting it out. Publishers who pass editing, design and printing costs on to you are **subsidy publishers**. Most are also **"vanity publishers"** who "accept" *anything* you submit. Vanity publishers are poorly regarded in the industry.

If you hope to sell your work directly to a publisher without going through an agent, study the submission guidelines on the publisher's website or call them to ask for guidelines. The annual guide, *Writer's Market,* lists helpful information about what publishers are interested in and what they *don't* want to see. Don't expect them to make an exception just for you.

5

CONTRACT

The big moment arrives: A "real" publisher offers you a book contract! Your first instinct may be to sign it as quickly as possible and shout, "Show me the money!" After all, most traditional publishers pay authors some sort of advance.

If you obtain your publishing contract through an agent, the agent should negotiate the best deal possible. Although many contracts are standard forms, you *can* negotiate to some extent. You just might get what you ask for!

I strongly urge you to ask for both title and cover approval. However, publishers often suggest titles that might bring more sales; don't rule out ideas you don't like without a good reason. The title and cover are crucial parts of marketing, so *do* make certain they reflect your book's content accurately. The cover image should reproduce well in black-and-white and in color, and the title must read well when it's reduced.

6

MANUSCRIPT

After celebrating the acceptance of your contract, it's time to get back to work! If you've written only a partial draft, complete it as rapidly as possible. Set it aside for a few days if you can and then return to revise and improve it. Writing can *always* be improved, so aim to write in a way that no one can misinterpret what you mean. Make every word count!

Share your revised draft with other writers. Try to work with some who have published before. (Chapter 18 suggests some ways to find them.) Incorporate whatever suggestions they offer that make sense to you and ignore any suggestions that don't. Your gut instinct will help you decide.

If possible, hire a professional editor — or *at the very least* a proofreader — to review your draft before submitting it to the editor at the publishing house. Don't rely on their editor to fix the problems. Polish your manuscript until it shines!

7

EDITORS

When you work with a traditional publisher, you'll likely work with one or more different types of editors.

Your primary editor at the publishing house will often be an **acquisitions editor** or a **developmental editor**. Such an editor addresses "big picture" aspects like content and organization and oversees the project throughout the entire publishing process. This editor may delete text that isn't working and/or ask you to add new text. He or she may also revise or reposition sentences, paragraphs or even chapters.

When your book is in its final draft, a **copyeditor** — most often an outside freelancer — will check the "picky little details" such as grammar, spelling and punctuation and may also make edits to enhance clarity and readability and to ensure that your book reflects the publisher's style. After the copyedit, the production staff takes over.

8

DESIGNERS, LAYOUT ARTISTS & PHOTOGRAPHERS

Books require two different types of designers — one designs the book cover and the other designs the internal pages. In some cases, one person does both jobs.

If your book has internal illustrations or photos, *you* will most likely be the one who must provide and pay for them. Children's picture book publishers, however, usually choose their own illustrators. Children's writers who send illustrations that the publisher doesn't like risk getting rejected.

If your book includes tables, graphs or charts, you usually provide the information and the layout artist formats them. If it includes photos or other illustrations, you must provide them.

Although it's said a picture is worth a thousand words, you'll usually need to describe the image or at least refer to it in the text of your book rather than just plop it in. You'll also need to indicate approximately where to insert it and write a caption for it. I say *approximately* because the editor or layout artist will determine its exact position.

Layout artists use special software, such as InDesign or QuarkXPress, to create the final pages of your book. Although you *can* lay out books in word processing programs like Microsoft Word, such programs lack the features that layout software has to fine-tune books.

Layout software allows greater control over text, images and page breaks. Layout artists can make fine adjustments to make text fit and improve your book's aesthetics.

Nearly every book includes an author photo on the cover, on the author bio page or both. Your photo doesn't have to be done in a studio by a professional photographer, but it does need to be shot in decent lighting, be sharply focused and be saved in the right format.

The best formats for printed materials are TIFFs (Tagged Image File Format) or JPGs/JPEGs (compressed image files named after the Joint Photographic Experts Group and pronounced jay-peg) with a dpi (dots per inch) resolution of 300 or more. For ebooks and websites, JPGs ranging from 72 to 300 dpi are fine. I suggest requesting photos in both TIFF and JPG formats at 300 dpi. For ebooks and websites, PDFs (Portable Document Files) often work as well. A PDF is like a snapshot that captures everything on the final page.

For promotion purposes, you'll also need a good image of your book's front cover. Your publisher should provide that. Again, request a TIFF and a JPG, though in many instances a PDF will suffice.

9

PRINTER

When your book's layout is complete and has been double-checked and proofread, it's ready to send to a printer.

Offset printers offer high quality but require a sizeable investment. To keep the cost per book down, many publishers print at least 5,000 books at a time.

Smaller print runs are increasingly printed through a **digital printer** or through **print on demand (POD)**. The quality doesn't quite match that of offset, but it's close enough. (An exception might be a coffee table book or a book with lots of internal photos or color images.) With POD, books get printed digitally as they are ordered, as few as one book at a time. The cost per book is higher, but the customer pays it.

10

PRINTED BOOK

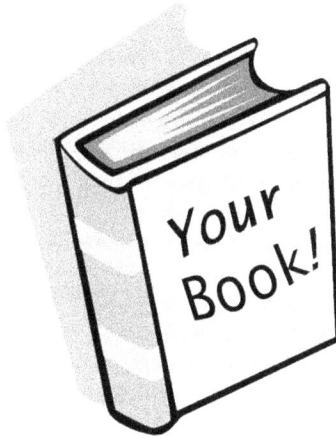

At last your "baby" has arrived! Once your book has been printed and bound, your publisher will most likely send you one of the first copies. There's nothing quite like the thrill of holding that first published book in your hand!

While many authors envision this point as the end of their journey, it's barely a halfway point. I hate to break that to you. ***You must get the word out that that new baby is available!*** If people don't know your book exists, they won't buy it.

A traditional publisher will help publicize your book to some extent, but *you* will have to do most of the work and pay most of the expenses. Your publisher may assign you a publicist, but he or she will usually be publicizing several books simultaneously. Don't expect much beyond a catalogue listing, some help writing and distributing news releases, sending out review copies and setting up some interviews.

News Release

A news release should be newsworthy, brief (1–2 double-spaced pages) and written in the third person, like a news story. Be sure to address who, what, when, where and why. Use letterhead or white or off-white paper and 12-point type.

- Type and center the words News Release in all caps.

- Skip about two lines. Then type For Immediate Release or a release date flush left.

- Type Contact: [Your Publicist's Name or Your Name, phone (with area code) and email address] flush right.

- Type and center an engaging 14-point headline about two lines below that. If you wish to, elaborate on the headline in a 12-point subhead.

- Type [Your City, State] in all caps flush left, followed by an em dash (wide dash). Continue with a stimulating hook.

- Introduce an issue or challenge that your book solves, or reveal the need for your book. Emphasize what makes your book unique and define your market(s). Then state how your book solves the issue or challenge or how it meets the need.

- Include order information: book title, publisher, month and year of publication, ISBN (International Standard Book Number), price and format (hardcover, softcover, ebook).

- Include a brief author bio.

- If you need a second page, type and center –more– at the bottom of the first page. End the release with –30– or ###.

- Type a call to action at the bottom like: [Your Name] is available for media interviews by phone, online or on location. Contact [Publicist's Name/him/her, phone number(s), email] to schedule an interview or to receive a review copy.

11

DISTRIBUTION

Once a book is ready to sell, it takes a few more folks to get it into your readers' hands.

Traditional publishers usually have well-established distribution channels for the books they publish. That's one major advantage of working with them.

Distributors are companies that market your book to bookstores, libraries, wholesalers and sometimes other retail outlets. The distributor's salespeople pitch the publisher's books and encourage booksellers to order them.

Wholesalers buy and warehouse large quantities of books and sell them directly to bookstores and libraries but do not send salespeople out to pitch the books they stock.

12

BOOKSTORES & LIBRARIES

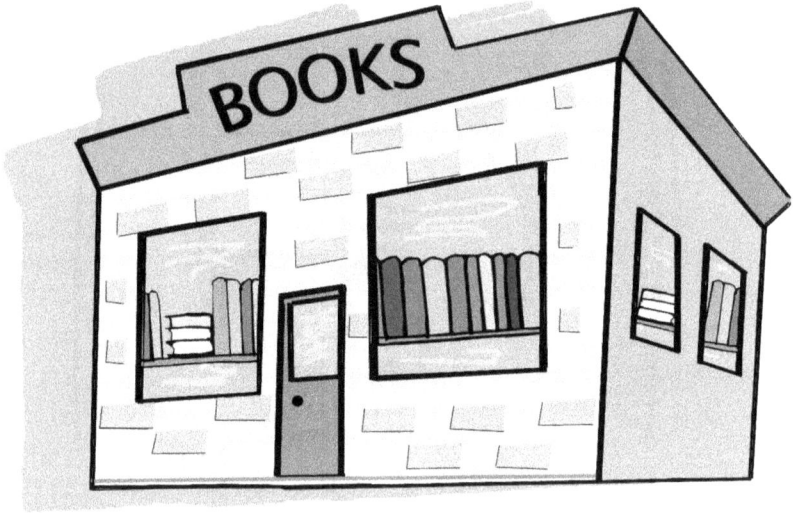

Books get into readers' hands both through brick-and-mortar (physical) and online bookstores and through libraries.

Books can also be sold through museums, associations, churches, gift shops, grocery stores, discount warehouses and other retail outlets. For instance, a cookbook might be sold through a kitchen supply store; a gardening book might be sold through a plant nursery; a health book might be sold through a hospital, a health food store or a supermarket.

Bookstores usually stock only books that they're allowed to return for credit. Because shelf space is limited, books that don't sell within a reasonably short period (around 90–120 days) are returned at the publisher's expense, and those returns are deducted from the author's account.

13

PROMOTION

Meet the Author!

If you're a new author, it may come as a surprise to learn that *you* must become the driving force to sell your books. It's not your agent's responsibility, your publisher's responsibility or even your distributor's responsibility. It's *yours*. After all, *you're* the authority on your book. You must find ways to make potential readers aware of and eager to buy your book.

Successful authors start thinking about, planning for and even promoting their book as soon as they get inspired to write it. Some spend their entire advance on promotion!

You can hire your own book publicist if you have the money. Most are pretty expensive, but having a publicist can increase your credibility. People tend to listen closer when someone else raves about your book than they do when you rave about it yourself. Publicists also maintain up-to-date databases and directories and have lots of media contacts already in place.

If you decide to hire a publicist, ensure that he or she will not only get the word out but also *follow up* with contacts for book reviews, interviews, excerpts and articles about you and your book. You don't want a news release or a review copy of your book to get lost in the shuffle.

Ask other writers to recommend a publicist. Find out what the publicist has done for other clients. Determine what he or she can do for you and within what timeframe. Be sure you check the publicist's references.

If you can't afford a publicist, consider hiring a college public relations or journalism student. Find an enthusiastic person with good research and telephone skills. You'll find a ton of promotion and publicity resources — some free and some paid — at www.bookmarket.com. Whenever you use a contact list, verify its information before you send something out. Any detail can change overnight.

Here are just few ideas for promoting your book:

• Have a website that you update regularly.

• Include your book title and order information in your email signature and on fax cover pages.

• Do interviews for both print and online magazines, newspapers, TV and radio.

• Write articles and blogs related to your book's subject.

• Do blog tours, podcasts, webinars and video book trailers.

See chapters 8, 14, 20, 25, 26 and 36 for other ideas.

14

DIRECT SALES

As an author, you don't have to — and shouldn't — rely on bookstores alone to sell your books. Book signings sponsored by bookstores can help, but not everyone who attends will buy a book. Fortunately, there are many other options.

Authors often offer talks and readings and sell their books at book clubs, libraries, schools, community meetings and nonprofit or professional conferences. Speaking before a well-targeted, captive audience often leads to good back-of-the-room book sales.

If you're uncomfortable speaking in public but are willing to learn how to do so, join a Toastmasters club, take a public speaking class or work with a professional coach.

15

INCOME/ROYALTIES

When working with a traditional publisher, your income comes from the advance and, provided the book is successful, royalties. The publisher is gambling on you, hoping you sell enough books to make a profit. Many books never do. You get part of your advance upon signing the contract and the balance upon acceptance and publication of the completed manuscript. Portions and timing of payments vary though.

Unless you're a celebrity, have a faithful following or have an especially interesting, timely and unique idea, don't expect a six-figure advance. These days an advance for a first book may run as low as $1,000. Many factors influence the size of an advance: the publisher, audience (adults, young adults, children), length, genre, format (hardcover or softcover), how unique and timely your book is and your marketing plans.

We'll explore the self-publishing pathway next.

The Self-Publishing Pathway

Manuscript

Editor

Designer, Layout Artist, Photographer

Distributor

Printer

Your Book!

Promotion

Meet the Author!

BOOKS

Bookstore/Library

Direct Sales

Income

16

NO QUERY, PROPOSAL OPTIONAL

To self-publish a book, whether printed and bound or ebook, there's no need to write a query letter because you won't be seeking an agent or a publisher. *You will be taking on all of the responsibility and expense of publishing your book* and — provided it sells well — reaping all of the rewards. You'll be running your own business. I recommend you study both Bernard Kamoroff's *Small Time Operator* and Dan Poynter's *Self-Publishing Manual* before plunging in.

It's not *necessary* to write a synopsis or a book proposal when you self-publish; however, I recommend that you do. Writing a synopsis forces you to think through your entire plot and helps you develop your characters. Writing a book proposal forces you to examine your book's organization, audience and competition and to plan marketing activities. It can also help you determine a reasonable price for your book.

17

NO AGENT, PUBLISHER OR CONTRACT

As I mentioned in chapter 16, you don't need a literary agent when you self-publish, and you don't need a publisher either. *You become the publisher,* so no book contract is involved.

As a self-publisher, you may contract with editors, designers, illustrators, layout artists, photographers, printers, distributors, wholesalers, bookstores, publicists and other services, but you don't contract with another publisher.

18

MANUSCRIPT

When you self-publish, you need to be especially attentive if you wish to produce a high-quality book. Even if the content of your book is riveting, nothing will turn off readers and ruin your credibility quicker than careless errors.

Because the mind tends to fill in what you're thinking — but may not have actually written — it's important to have others read, critique and edit your work — even if you're a professional editor. No one is perfect.

Although friends and family may have some helpful suggestions, they won't be able to give unbiased opinions. You're better off having other writers — particularly professional published writers — read and critique your work. You can find other writers by joining writers' organizations or local or online critique groups or by meeting them in person through writing classes, workshops or conferences.

19

EDITORS

I recommend that *everyone* hire at least one editor when publishing a book. Ideally, you should work with both a developmental editor and a copyeditor. If that's not possible, opt for the copyeditor *after* several other writers have read your book. If that's not possible, at least hire a proofreader. Skipping the editorial work invariably results in an inferior book. Traditionally published books go through several editing and proofreading passes, and errors can still slip through.

To find good editors, get other writers' recommendations or contact the Editorial Freelancers Association. Look for editors who specialize in or have experience with your genre. Ask them for samples of their work, and get client references. Many will edit a few sample pages of your manuscript for free.

Once the final edit is done, you might want to register your copyright if you haven't already: www.copyright.gov

20

DESIGNERS, LAYOUT ARTISTS & PHOTOGRAPHERS

Unless you have excellent book design skills yourself, also hire a book designer and a layout artist. A striking cover design is especially important. Although it's often said that you can't judge a book by its cover, I assure you, people do.

Warning: An artist with no book industry experience may be unaware of specifications required for books. The trim size, spine width, color setting, resolution, file types and programs used to lay out a book and design its cover will vary with the printing service and the paper you choose.

If your book appears in brick-and-mortar bookstores and libraries, the spine may be all a reader sees. Make it count!

21

PRINTER

Just as with traditional publishing, when your book's layout is complete and has been double-checked and proofread, it's ready to send to the printer.

When you're self-publishing, printing your book through an offset printer means a sizeable investment. To keep the price per book down, you'll usually have to print at least 1,000 — for several thousand dollars. Use digital printing for shorter runs.

Unless you're fairly certain you can sell all the books you print within a year, I suggest that you first consider print on demand (POD). It's quick and inexpensive for you as the publisher, and if your sales take off, you can print additional books through an offset or digital printer later.

Warning: A lot of Internet companies call themselves "POD publishers" or "self-publishers," hoping to be perceived as traditional publishers. They're rarely worth the money. Watch out for those who offer lots of pricey "packages."

Three reputable POD companies are CreateSpace, Lightning Source and BookBaby. Use others carefully.

The following list describes some information you must know when contracting with any type of printer.

• **Trim size:** Width x height of the finished book — 6 x 9 inches is a common standard, but there are many other sizes.

• **Total page count:** Number of laid-out pages, *including front matter* (title page, copyright page, table of contents, etc.) *and back matter* (author bio, index, order form, etc.).

• **Cover type:** Hardcover or softcover (paperback).

• **Binding:** In perfect bound books (the most common for softcovers) the cover wraps around the pages and is glued to the spine. Hardcovers may be sewn (cloth bound or case bound) or glued (perfect bound case bound) and may or may not have a dust jacket (a protective wrap-around paper cover).

• **Paper:** Text stock is usually uncoated 50-, 55- or 60-lb. white or off-white (though photos look better on coated stock). Cover stock may be coated or matte 10- or 12-pt. stock. To keep costs down, use a printer's "house stock" (paper bought in large quantities and kept onsite).

• **Ink:** Choose either black or 4-color (CMYK). CMYK combines set percentages of cyan/blue (C), magenta/red (M), yellow (Y) and black (K) to produce any color.

• **File types:** Most commonly, text files are InDesign or QuarkXPress files. Image files are TIFFs, JPGs or PDFs (as discussed in chapter 8).

22

PRINTED BOOK

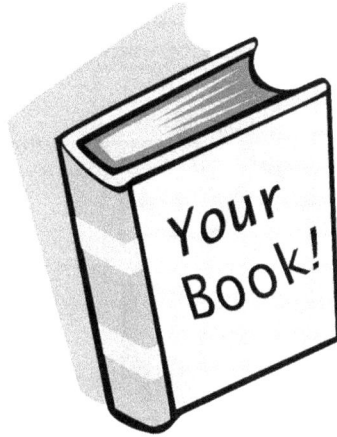

As with traditional publishing, it's a thrill to hold a printed copy of your own book in your hands — sometimes more so. And with self-publishing there's even more work ahead of you.

If you've invested in a large print run, you'll have to work hard and fast to sell your inventory. If you have books left to sell at the end of the year — at least in the United States — you'll owe taxes on that inventory.

As a self-publisher and a businessperson, you also need to pay attention to sales taxes, as well as federal and often state and local taxes. You may need to obtain a sales tax permit, which allows you to print books tax-free. You then charge and collect tax on your sales and pay those taxes regularly. Check the requirements in your state and city before you begin self-publishing. Contact your state comptroller's office or talk with an accountant.

23

DISTRIBUTION

One disadvantage of self-publishing a book through offset or digital printing is that it's often hard to get good distribution.

It's much easier for distributors and wholesalers to work with large accounts, so a self-publisher with just one or two titles won't interest them much. I therefore suggest joining the Independent Book Publishers Association or the Small Publishers Association of North America — not just for the publishing and marketing information — but also for the distribution benefits. These organizations have special partnerships and co-op programs with wholesalers and distributors like Ingram, Baker & Taylor, Small Press United and Quality Books.

24

BOOKSTORES & LIBRARIES

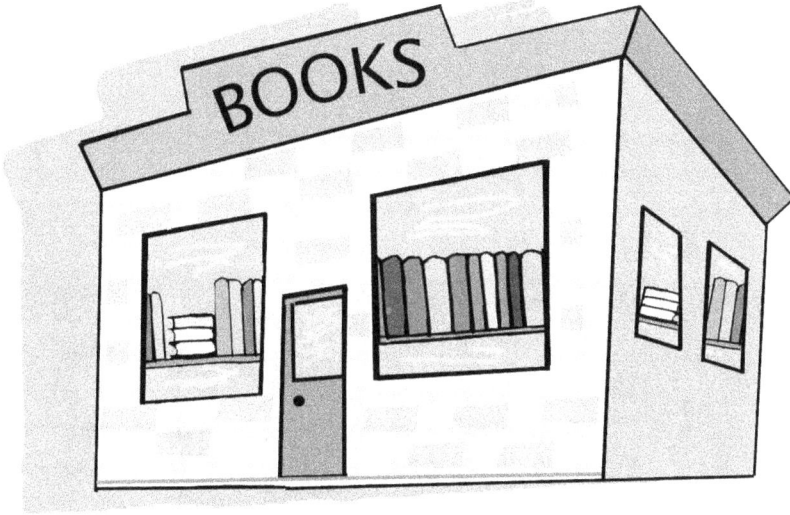

Without a distributor or wholesaler, getting into bookstores may present a challenge. Some bookstores simply won't deal with self-publishers, but some accept books on consignment.

Most every place in the book trade will require an ISBN (International Standard Book Number). An ISBN identifies a book or book-like product (like an audiobook) and its publisher. *You'll need a separate ISBN for each edition or format of your book.* If you use print on demand, many POD companies offer free ISBNs if you list *them* as the publisher. To list yourself as the publisher in the U.S. or its territories, obtain a SAN (Standard Address Number). Unless your book is an ebook, you'll also need a bar code. You can purchase ISBNs, bar codes and a SAN from www.Bowker.com.

25

PROMOTION

Meet the Author!

As a self-published author, you have most of the same promotion opportunities and challenges as a traditionally published author. You may have a harder time getting bookstores to sponsor signings though. Most bookstores won't do so unless they stock your books.

Some book reviewers won't review self-published books, but others will. Remember, getting a review can take several months, and review space is quite limited. There are plenty of other options for promotion though — sometimes too many!

Plenty of self-publishers build a great following these days by using websites and social media: blogging, tweeting and interacting on FaceBook, LinkedIn and the like.

26

DIRECT SALES

As a self-published author, you may also often sell directly to your customers. Always carry business cards, flyers or brochures with order information and your book's cover image. If the cover image won't fit, try to match its color scheme.

Sales can happen anytime, so always carry a book or two with you. Keep a case of books in your car and keep cash available for making change.

If you have a mobile phone or an iPad, look into Square, Intuit's GoPayment or PayPal Here. These nifty devices plug into your phone or iPad and allow you to swipe credit cards on the spot. Each swipe costs you around 2–2.75% of the purchase price, and the balance goes to your bank account.

27

INCOME

Once you've paid the expenses for publishing a book, the income your sales produce is *all yours*. No agent or publisher takes any percentage of the profits. However, if you work with a distributor or wholesaler, have someone else fulfill book orders or sell through bookstores or other retail outlets, they'll receive some sort of percentage. Set your prices accordingly.

The real trick is paying off the expenses. Using print on demand (POD) rather than printing a large run with an offset or digital printer makes a lot of sense for a self-publisher. So does publishing an ebook. Neither POD nor ebook publishing requires a large investment. These methods also offer a ready way to sell books without seeking a distributor or wholesaler. For most self-publishers, I recommend trying both. As with other services, though, you need to do your homework first.

Now we'll explore the ebook publishing pathway.

The Ebook Publishing Pathway

Manuscript

Designer, Photographer

Editor

Online Distributor

Conversion Service

BOOKS

Promotion

Meet the Author!

Bookstore/Library

Your Book!

Ebook

Direct Sales

Income

28

NO QUERY, PROPOSAL OPTIONAL

As with self-publishing a printed and bound book, self-publishing an ebook requires no query letter or book proposal, though writing a book proposal is helpful.

You can publish an **ebook (electronic or digital book)** before, after, simultaneously with or even without a printed version. To date, ebooks offer the quickest and least expensive way to get a book into a reader's hands. Ebooks are increasingly popular and can be read on a variety of devices. The Kindle, Nook, Sony Reader, Kobo, Diesel, iPad, computer screen and many cell phones are just a few of the options available.

Because ebook sales are rising so rapidly, many people think ebooks will soon bring an end to printed books. I doubt that printed books will ever become obsolete though. That's comparable to thinking TV would replace radio.

29

NO AGENT, PUBLISHER OR CONTRACT

Again, no literary agent, publisher or book contract is involved when you publish an ebook. You may still contract with editors, designers, illustrators and photographers. But rather than a layout artist you may need to hire someone to prepare your manuscript for conversion for various ebook reading devices. If you're fairly computer savvy, though, you can do this yourself. Chapter 30 describes the basics.

30

MANUSCRIPT

The manuscript for an ebook is much the same as that for a printed book; however, the page layout usually differs and can frequently be done in Microsoft Word.

There are no fixed pages within the text of most ebooks because ebook reading devices allow readers to adjust the font size of text, thereby changing how much of the page appears on the screen. (Ebooks in PDF format are one exception.) You can, however, force page breaks after front matter pages or at the end of chapters by using Microsoft Word's Insert / Break / Page Break command. Don't type extra paragraph returns on one page to go to the next because that can create blank pages in the ebook.

There's no point in having page numbers, headers (repeating text at the top of the page, like the book title) or footers (repeating text at the bottom of the page, like the page number) in an ebook either. However, in case you want to print the manuscript to review it, I suggest leaving page numbers in until it has been edited and then removing them just before submitting the book for conversion.

Except for PDFs and iBooks, font choices are often limited as well. Stick with something simple like Arial, Garamond or Times New Roman. You can still use bold, italics, underlines, all caps or centered text or vary the size of fonts. Use 11- to 12-point type for most text and 14–18 point for titles and headings. Avoid bullets and symbols; they often convert to question marks. Set up character styles using Word's Format / Style command, not its Format / Font command.

Many ebook reading devices can't handle extra spaces, tabs, columns or tables, so avoid them as well. To indent paragraphs, set up a paragraph style using Word's Format / Style command, not its Format / Paragraph command. Don't use tabs or spaces to indent them. You may need to convert multi-column pages and tables and graphs to PDFs and treat them like illustrations.

Some ebook reading devices can't display illustrations or photos yet or can do so on an extremely limited basis, so try to describe their contents as text. If you use illustrations or photos, embed them in your Word file using the Insert / Photo / Picture from File command, center them and set them to wrap In Line with Text.

Formatting a Word file in preparation to convert it to an ebook isn't all that difficult if you follow the conversion service or online bookstore's style guide carefully. Smashwords has an excellent style guide for most ebook reading devices: www.Smashwords.com

If you wish to create an ebook for Apple's iPad, check out the free iBooks Author application from www.Apple.com.

31

EDITORS

Again, I suggest hiring an editor. Although it's much faster to produce an ebook than a printed book, that's no reason to skimp on quality. Rushing to get an ebook out without a careful edit will likely lead to bad reviews and resentful readers.

To better serve your needs, try to find an editor who has experience with ebooks. Some elements that commonly appear in printed books may need to be moved to other places or may not be needed at all. For instance, because ebook readers tend to want to jump right in, the copyright page, acknowledgements and author bio might appear at the end of an ebook rather than at the beginning. Tables of contents may be omitted or may contain hyperlinks for readers to click to jump to specific chapters or sections. Indexes might be omitted altogether since most ebooks are searchable.

32

DESIGNERS & PHOTOGRAPHERS, NO LAYOUT ARTISTS NEEDED

On most ebook reading devices, the internal pages of the ebook are formatted more simply than those of a printed book.

Because not all ebooks include covers, a reader who downloads your book may see your cover image only on the online bookstore site. That doesn't mean your cover isn't important. It can still influence an ebook reader's purchase.

As mentioned in chapter 30, except for PDFs and iBooks, you must treat illustrations and photos differently in ebooks. If you include illustrations and photos, insert them above or below text but not next to it. And remember that many ebook reading devices display images only in black, white and grays.

33

PRINTER (CONVERSION SERVICE)

With an ebook, the "printer" is actually a conversion service or **aggregator.** Such a service converts your final book file to a file or files that one or more ebook reading devices can display. A single company may run both a conversion service and an online bookstore. A few aggregators I recommend are Smashwords, Kindle Direct Publishing, PubIt! and BookBaby.

As with POD, readers order directly from the online bookstore, pay them and then download your book.

Warning: You can also sell ebooks directly from your own website, in which case you must collect any applicable taxes and file and pay them. You may also want digital rights management. (See chapter 35.) I prefer to avoid the hassle.

34

EBOOK

Some self-publishers first publish their book as an ebook. Others publish the ebook without publishing a printed book.

Before you officially release your ebook, check the final version carefully. If you don't have an ebook reading device, download a simulated ebook reader from your conversion service to view the book as it will appear to your customers on their devices.

Warning: Currently, if you wish to sell ebooks through Apple's online bookstore, you're required to end the price with 99 cents. (Don't ask me about the logic for this. Just do it.)

Note that different formats of the same book require different ISBN numbers, so you'll need two ISBNs if you're also publishing a printed book. You can obtain ISBNs from www.Bowker.com. You won't need a bar code for an ebook though because the final product can't be scanned.

35

DISTRIBUTION TO ONLINE BOOKSTORES & LIBRARIES

Because ebooks are downloaded from online sites — even from library sites — distribution is handled for you (at least to some extent). Some online bookstores offer "extended distribution plans" to get your ebooks out to other sites. These plans sometimes have some restrictions. Be careful.

While I'm talking about distribution, I'll explain a bit about **digital rights management (DRM)** — the technology used to enable secure distribution of copyrighted digital material. DRM is meant to prevent illegal copying.

Online bookstores differ on DRM philosophies. Some don't offer DRM at all. If you're concerned about pirating, go with one that does; otherwise, you'll just have to trust people to not share copies of your book.

My own philosophy is that folks who pirate things will probably find a way to get around any technological barrier. I just get my work out there and try not to worry about it.

36

PROMOTION

Meet the Author!

Okay, you won't be signing your ebook at a bookstore. In fact you probably won't sign it at all. But that doesn't mean you don't need to promote it! You can still use many of the same promotion options as you would with a printed book (chapters 8, 13, 14, 20, 25 and 26). Plus you'll get another *great* option.

To help customers decide if they want to purchase a book, online bookstores have been offering peeks inside for years. Online bookstores also give ebook authors the option to let readers sample their work. When you upload an ebook to an online bookstore, you're usually asked what percentage of the book you'd like to offer as a sample. Aim to provide just enough to get a reader hooked and aching to read more. Sampling is not only a great sales tool, but it's free!

37

DIRECT SALES FROM YOUR SITE

Although you won't have a physical product to sell when you publish an ebook, you *can* choose to let customers buy and download ebook files directly from your site rather than from an online bookstore.

Warning: Ensure that selling from your site doesn't break your agreement with the conversion service.

If you want to sell ebooks directly from your website, you'll need a way to accept credit cards. Similar to Square, Intuit's GoPayment or PayPal Here, companies like Clickbank and PayPal allow you to accept credit cards from your website without setting up a traditional merchandise account that requires a monthly fee or minimum number of sales.

38

INCOME

When you self-publish an ebook, just as when you self-publish a printed and bound book, *any money you make once you've paid off your expenses is yours to keep.* And, fortunately, ebook publishing brings very few expenses!

* * *

That covers the major "pit stops" of publishing by following the three pathways currently available: traditional publishing, self-publishing printed books and self-publishing ebooks.

I hope you've learned enough to decide with reasonable confidence what's best for you and your books. Remember, there are no sure things in life (except death and taxes, of course). Just do your homework and give it your best shot!

If you still don't know which pathway to follow, chapter 39 lists further considerations that may help you decide.

39

CHOOSING YOUR PATHWAY(S)

I suggest that you weigh what's most important to you and most logical for your budget, your personality and your book. Think carefully about *why* you want to publish in the first place, and then review this list.

- For the **most prestige**, seek a traditional publisher.

- For the **best distribution**, seek a traditional publisher.

- For the **highest quality**, use an offset printer.

- For high quality with **less investment**, print digitally.

- For high quality with **even less investment**, use POD.

- For the **lowest investment** possible, publish an ebook.

- For the most **creative control** over the final product, self-publish a printed book.

- For the **longest time in print**, self-publish.

- For the **greatest speed**, publish an ebook.

- For **reasonably high speed**, go with POD.

- To **avoid many of the hassles** that come with running a business, seek a traditional publisher or self-publish only through POD and/or ebooks.

- For the **deepest satisfaction**, *go with your heart!*

For more information about publishing, check out my website and blog: www.castlecommunications.com

Best wishes on your journey! *— Lana*

ABOUT THE AUTHOR

Lana Castle is an editor, publishing consultant and teacher with a diverse background and over 30 years' experience in communications and publishing. She edits and develops printed books, ebooks and media materials for her clients. Lana is also an internationally published author of three other trade books:

Style Meister: The Quick-Reference Custom Style Guide (Castle Communications, 1998)

Bipolar Disorder Demystified: Mastering the Tightrope of Manic Depression (Da Capo/Perseus Books/Marlowe & Company, 2003)

Finding Your Bipolar Muse: How to Master Depressive Droughts & Manic Floods & Access Your Creative Power (Da Capo/Perseus Books/Marlowe & Company, 2006)

Lana lives in Austin, Texas with her husband Ralph, her bipolar cat Sylvia, two delightful tabbies — Sammy and Bob — and assorted tropical fish. She also has two wonderful "step-adults": Tom, a Tai Chi school owner, and Joy, a film director.

ACKNOWLEDGMENTS

I'd like to thank the Writers' League of Texas for all of the excellent meetings, classes, workshops, conferences and critique groups the organization sponsors. They have given and continue to give me an invaluable education.

I'd also like to thank my many wonderful clients and the participants in my publishing workshops at Austin Community College, the Writers' League of Texas and elsewhere over the years. Your questions and feedback have helped tremendously in the development of this book.

Finally, I'd like to thank my editor Loy White and my friends, family and supporters: Will Richards, Debbie Simms, Annie Berry, Dawn Sachse, Anita Ernest, Chin-Hsien C. Yang, Dayna Finet, Sara Puig Laas, Carol Pierce-Davis, Kay Coon, Jo Osborne and Ralph, Tom and Joy Gohring.

* * *

www.ingramcontent.com/pod-product-compliance
Lightning Source LLC
Chambersburg PA
CBHW071853020426

42331CB00007B/1982